How Delicious Is Baking Cookies!

50 Recipes to Enjoy the Satisfaction of Baking the Best and Richest Variety of Cookies at Home

By

American Chef's Table

Table of Contents

Introduction

Regardless of your expertise in the kitchen, when you are going to prepare cookies it is important to know certain tricks to get the best results, and even if you are a housewife, a pastry chef, or the best baker in the neighborhood, applying tricks when baking those delicious recipes for cookies, cakes, bread, pies, will definitely make a difference.

First of all, remember to be very clear about the recipes to be prepared and make sure you have all the necessary ingredients at hand, lest in the middle of the preparation, we realize that some ingredient is missing and we have to run out to buy it. Although this is an easy inconvenience to solve, it also takes time and delays the preparation of those coveted cookies to accompany the coffee at snack time.

Likewise, the best ingredients should always be chosen, in order to have the desired quality and flavor. If you have doubts about any ingredient, it is good to consult the information about it.

Another aspect to take into account is that the oven should not be overloaded. It is best to bake one tray of cookies at a time, on the medium oven rack. If you need to bake more than one tray at a time, swap positions of the top and bottom trays halfway through baking so that they bake and brown evenly.

Finally, before any preparation, the oven should be preheated for at least 15 minutes, so that when the tray enters the oven, it already has the necessary temperature and the estimated baking time is not exceeded, leaving the cookies too soft or burnt.

Do not wait then to prepare the delicious recipes below.

Chapter 1. Holiday Favorites

1. Chocolate Chip Cookie Dough Special K-Bars

(Ready in about 3 hours 15 minutes | serving 12 |Difficulty: Moderate)

Per serving: Kcal 267, Fat: 5g, Net Carbs: 39g, Protein: 6g

Ingredients

For Special K-bar

- 1 cup of brown rice syrup

- 1 cup of peanut butter

- 1/2 of sugar

- 4 1/2 cups corn flakes

For cookie dough

- 2 cups of salted cashews roasted

- 1/2 cup of unsalted whole pecans

- 2 teaspoons of sugar

- 2 teaspoons of sugar

- 1/2 teaspoons melted butter

- 2 tablespoons of pure vanilla extract

- 1/2 cup of micro chocolate chips

- 2 1/2 cups Dark chocolate chips

Method

1. Oiled a 9-13-inch Pyrex pan.

2. Place the cashews and pecans in a food processor and process until a smooth nut butter resembles the mixture, stopping if appropriate to scratch down the cup's surface. This can take between 5 and 10 minutes to process, so be careful.

3. Sugar, butter, and vanilla are extracted. The sweeteners can thicken the nut butter quite a little at first, but keep grinding, and gradually, the heat can melt the sugar and smooth the nut butter away. Again, if it already seems too dense, continue processing

4. This is the challenging part — you need to pop it into the fridge to cool until the nut butter is done processing. The chocolate chips will melt straight into the almond butter and transform it brown if you don't chill it. When it's

chilled, stir in the mini chocolate chips for around 25 minutes.

5. In a big saucepan, blend peanut butter, brown rice syrup, and sugar altogether as the "bread dough" is cooling off. Heat nearly to a boil, taking caution not to smoke. Switch off the heat and apply the corn flakes to the mix.

6. Spread an even layer until the cookie dough is ready.

7. Melt the chocolate chips (mine in the microwave, heat for 30 seconds on maximum strength, stir, stir again for 30 seconds, and stir until melted). Over the cookie dough, place the molten chocolate and spread it out in an even layer. Refrigerate it for at least 2 hours. Let the bars remain at room temperature for 15 minutes until they are removed.

2. Triple-Layer Peanut Butter, Chocolate Chip Cookie, and Cookie Dough Cups

(Ready in about 3 hours 20 minutes | serving 12 |Difficulty: Hard)

Per serving: Kcal 164, Fat: 8g, Net Carbs: 19g, Protein: 2g

Ingredients

For chocolate chip cookie:

- 1 1/4 cups All-purpose flour

- 1/2 tsp of baking soda

- 1/2 tsp of salt

- 1 teaspoon of water

- 1/2 cup melted unsalted butter, 1 stick

- 1/4 cup of sugar granulated

- 1/2 cup of boxed brown sugar

- 2 teaspoons of vanilla extract

- 1 large egg

- 1 semi-sweet cup of chocolate chips

For the cookie dough:

- 1 piece of butter (1/2 cup)

- 1/2 cup of brown sugar

- 2 tablespoons of coconut milk

- 1 teaspoon vanilla extract

- 3/4 cup of flour

- 1/4 teaspoon of salt

- 1/2 cup of micro chocolate chips

For peanut butter:

- 1 cup of peanut butter

- 1/2-1 teaspoon vanilla extract

- 20 ounces chocolate

Method

1. To make some cookies cover a 9x15 inch baking sheet with parchment paper.

2. In a bowl, combine the baking soda, flour, and salt. In a wide mixer cup, beat the brown sugar, butter, vanilla extract, and granulated sugar until smooth, around 3 to 5 minutes. Add the egg and whisk well. Mix in the flour mixture and 1 teaspoon of water, gently. Mix in the crisps with cookies. In the prepared bowl, press the crust into it.

3. Bake for 10 to 15 minutes, until the cookies are only placed on top. Before cutting, cool, ideally overnight, or at least two hours, or if time is a challenge, 50 minutes in the fridge.

4. In the meantime, make cups of cocoa. Melt approximately 12 ounces of cocoa in a healthy microwave bowl for 30 seconds, swirling each time, until molten and smooth. In cupcake molds, position 12 cupcake trays. Smooth the cocoa up the sides of the liners by using the slotted spoon or a pastry brush. Place 10 minutes in the refrigerator or 20 minutes in the fridge.

5. Form the cookie dough until the cookies are frozen and ready to go. In a wide mixing bowl, put the butter in the tray of a standing mixer. Add the brown sugar, vanilla, and coconut milk or cream to the dish. Beat when mixed in color, fuzzy and bright. Add the salt and flour when mixed. Stir in the crisps with cookies. Put back, cut the cookie dough and add it to a fresh bowl.

6. Mix the cookie dough in the same bowl and stir and mix the vanilla and peanut butter. Mix until mixed and smooth.

7. Pick the cooled cookies to assemble the cups, cut off the very outer edges to preserve them for eating, and then split the cookie horizontally into 6 rows. Split any row into four squares, then. You have to have twenty-four cookie squares now. Remember that only 12 cookie squares are needed, so either save the remainder for food or produce 12 more cups or halve the cookie recipe.

8. Pick the chocolate cup from the refrigerator now. Place a cookie at the bottom of each one when dealing with the chocolate cups already in the cupcake molds. Over the cookie, spread a sheet of cookie dough and then a layer of peanut butter.

9. Melt the remaining chocolate in a safe microwave bowl at intervals of 30 seconds, stirring each time, until melted and smooth. Spoon the chocolate gently over the peanut butter coating that hides the peanut butter.

10. Before serving, place in the fridge for at least thirty minutes.

11. These can be kept in a cold place but are better stored in the fridge right away.

3. Brown Sugar and Pineapple Roasted Acorn Squash with Spiced Brown Butter

(Ready in about 3 hours 20 minutes | serving 12 |Difficulty: Moderate)

Per serving: Kcal 189, Fat: 6g, Net Carbs: 36g, Protein: 2g

Ingredients

- 2 wedges of acorn squash

- 2 cups of brown sugar

- 1 (8.5 ounces) pineapple

- Salt and pepper

- 6 tablespoons of LAND O' LAKES

- 1 1/2 teaspoons of cinnamon

- 1 1/2 teaspoons of chili powder

- 1 pomegranate

Method

1. Preheat oven to 425 ° F. Grease a 9x13 inch baking dish lightly with softened butter.

2. Remove the seeds, halve all acorn squash, but preserve them for roasting, then cut the squash into wedges. Line up the wedges of squash in the prepared plate. Sprinkle the brown sugar generously over the squash, then season with salt and pepper. Now spoon the smashed pineapple over the squash wedges, causing the squash wedges' cavity to be filled by some of the pineapples while the remainder of the pineapple collects around the squash.

3. In a small saucepan placed over medium fire, add the butter until just browned. The butter, foam, and froth will melt so that the bottom will begin to brown. Remove from the fire and whisk off the bottom of the pan with the browned butter pieces. Whisk together the cinnamon, sugar, and chili powder. Using your palms to brush all over the squash, spill the butter over the squash. Using plastic, cover the dish, and put it in the oven. Roast for 30 minutes or until the squash is soft and caramelized, then peel the foil and bake for more than 30 minutes.

4. Sprinkle toasted acorn squash seeds and pomegranate arils with the squash.

5. Rinse them off and pat them dry to roast your stored acorn squash seeds. Add 1 tablespoon of olive oil, salt, and pepper. Put 400 degrees F in the oven and roast for 10 minutes or until brown and toasted golden.

4. Eight Ingredient Irish Coffee Fudge Brownies

(Ready in about 35 minutes | serving 16 |Difficulty: Easy)

Per serving: Kcal 149, Fat: 7g, Net Carbs: 19g, Protein: 2g

Ingredients

- 1 stick (1/2 cup) salted butter

- 3/4 cup sugar granulated

- 1/4 cup of Baileys Irish Cream

- 2 teaspoons of vanilla extract

- 2 large eggs

- 3/4 cup chocolate

- 1/2 cup all-purpose flour

- 1-2 teaspoons Instant coffee granules

- 1/2 cup chocolate semi-sweet chips

Methods

1. The oven should be preheated to 350 degrees F. With parchment paper, cover an 8x8 inch baking dish.

2. Mix butter, baileys, honey, vanilla, and eggs in a medium bowl until mixed. Include the starch, chocolate, and coffee powder and whisk until just blended. Stir in the chocolate chips, if necessary. In the prepared plate, distribute the batter uniformly. Transfer to the oven and cook for 20-25 minutes or until you have just arranged the brownies. Let it cool, then break it into pieces.

3. Melt 1/2 cup of chocolate chips and 1/4-1/2 cup of Baileys together until smooth and mixed, if a chocolate drizzle is needed.

5. The Very Best Peanut Butter Cup Fudge Brownies

(Ready in about 1 hour 15 minutes | serving 16 | Difficulty: Easy)

Per serving: Kcal 628, Fat: 31g, Net Carbs: 85g, Protein: 7g

Ingredients

- 10 teaspoons of unsalted butter

- 4 ounces of milk chocolate

- 1 cup of sugar granulated

- 2 teaspoons Instant coffee

- 2 teaspoons of vanilla extract

- 2 large eggs

- 1/2 cup of cocoa powder

- 1/2 cup all-purpose flour

- 1/4 teaspoon of kosher salt

- 1/2 cup of peanut butter

- 1 tablespoon butter

- 1 tablespoon of sugar powder

For fudge frosting:

- 1/2 cup of heavy cream

- 5 1/2 ounces of sweet chocolate

- 1 tablespoon of peanut butter

- 2 teaspoons of vanilla

- 1 tablespoon of bourbon

Method

1. Cover an 8x8 inch baking tray with parchment paper, enabling the sides from the pan such that the brownies can be taken out later quickly. To 350 degrees F, preheat the oven.

2. In a medium-size bowl that is microwave-proof, add the butter and 2 ounces of milk chocolate. Microwave butter and chocolate at intervals of 30 seconds, stirring until melting and smooth after each interval. Add the instant coffee and sugar to the melting chocolate mixture and whisk until fully mixed. Add the vanilla, then the eggs, whisk until smooth. Then whisk in the flour, salt, and cocoa powder until just blended and smooth. Remember not to over-mix the batter; it's going to be dense.

3. Mix all the peanut butter, butter, and powdered sugar in another tiny mixing bowl until smooth.

4. Pour half the brownie into the prepared skillet with the batter. Dollop the mixture of peanut butter into the brownie batter and brush with the leftover 2 ounces of sliced chocolate. Now layer on top of all the other layers with the leftover batter. Spread the batter gently on the edges, if appropriate. Don't panic if the whole surface region isn't filled with all the batter; it will even out when the brownies bake.

5. Bake until the brownies are placed on top for 25-30 minutes. Before frosting, cause the brownies to cool thoroughly.

6. Meanwhile, heat the milk in a saucepan to just under a simmer to create the frosting. Stir in the peanut butter and chocolate until melting and smooth. Add the bourbon and vanilla until nice and fluffy. When the brownies are cold enough to frost, put the frosting aside.

7. Place the frosting on top until the brownies are finished. Sprinkle sliced Reese's in it. Enable about 30 minutes to set the frosting, then slice into bars. Brownies may be frozen for around four days at room temperature or in the refrigerator.

6. Chocolate Lovers Triple-Layer Coffee Caramel Chocolate Mousse Cake

(Ready in about 3 hours 25 minutes | serving 6 |Difficulty: Hard)

Per serving: Kcal 1036, Fat: 56g, Net Carbs: 90g, Protein: 11g

Ingredients

For the chocolate cake:

- 1 1/8 cups wheat

- 1/3 cup cocoa powder

- 1/2 cup sugar

- 1/2 teaspoon salt

- 3/4 teaspoon baking soda

- 3/4 teaspoon baking powder

- 1 egg

- 1/2 cup buttermilk

- 1/4 cup of canola oil

- 2 tablespoons vanilla extract

- 1/4 cup of warm coffee

- Kahlua 2-4 teaspoons

For the chocolate mousse:

- 12 ounces chocolate

- 4 teaspoons butter

- 2 teaspoons water

- 4 egg yolks

- 1 tablespoon sugar

- 2 teaspoons water

- 3 cups frozen heavy cream

For chocolate coffee caramel:

- 1/4 cup water

- 1/2 cup sugar

- 1 cup milk

- 1/4 cup of coffee

- 2 scoops of chocolate chips

- 1 tablespoon vanilla

Method

1. Preheat oven to 355 ° F to bake the cake. A circular 9x9 baking dish or a 9-inch cake pan is oiled.

2. In a big cup, whisk together the chocolate, flour, sugar, baking soda, baking powder, and salt. Add the oil, buttermilk, vanilla, and eggs. Beat the mixer at a medium pace for two minutes. Beat the coffee in it. Spread the batter uniformly into the prepared baking dish and bake in the middle for 25 minutes. Remove the dish and leave five minutes to cool. Then scratch the cake with a fork all over it and spill the Kahlua equally. Cover and store in the freezer with the baking bowl.

3. To produce chocolate mousse, add the butter, chocolate, and 2 tablespoons of water to a secure microwave dish. Microwave at intervals of 30 seconds, swirling with each one, until smooth and molten. To cool, set aside. Stir together all the egg yolks, sugar, and 2 teaspoons of water in a shallow saucepan. Place over medium heat on the stove and whisk until the mixture thickens marginally and the back of a spoon is simply covered around 2-3 minutes. Stir in the egg mix with the molten chocolate

until it is fully smooth. Place the cream in the refrigerator as you whisk it.

4. In the bowl of the stand mixer, place cream and whip until rigid peaks develop. Making sure you should not over-beat, then the cream gets lumpy. Now add the cooled chocolate mixture to half of the whipped cream. Slowly pour the cream into the chocolate until no further stripes exist. Add the leftover cream, then add it into the mousse softly. Place it in a refrigerator.

5. Now apply to a new bowl the leftover cream and whip it exactly as you did before. Add 1/2 teaspoon of powdered sugar until whipped, then whip once blended. Place it in a refrigerator.

6. Create a caramel chocolate coffee, whisk together a little bowl of heavy cream and vanilla. Mix the sugar and water over medium to high heat in a shallow saucepan. Get it to a simmer in the mixture. Watch and whisk before the mixture begins tasting like sugar and changes to a golden hue, and then to a medium brown as it starts to simmer. It's going to take 5-6 minutes. Slowly add in the cream mixture until you see that it has begun to turn brown, whisking constantly and steadily. Around the whisk, the sugar will harden. Don't worry; it will melt. Continue to whisk. Continue to heat until the mixture has thickened

and is a light color of caramel, around 5 minutes more (do not allow it to get so thick, when it rests, it can thicken). Remove the beans, chocolate chips, and vanilla from the heat and stir in.

7. Line up six glasses or glass jars to arrange the cakes. Drizzle with 1 tablespoon of coffee caramel at the bottom of each pot, then crumble into a cake sheet. Then add a sheet of mouse and a whipped cream layer, sprinkle it with another tablespoon or two caramel. To end with a layer of whipped cream, replicate the layers two more times. Then add the crumbled cake and drizzle with more caramel sauce on top of the whipped cream. Cool for 2 hours or before fit for serving.

7. Toasted Coconut Cream Rum Chocolate Mousse Crepe Cake

(Ready in about 3 hours 20 minutes | serving 8 |Difficulty: Hard)

Per serving: Kcal 593, Fat: 38g, Net Carbs: 46g, Protein: 16g

For crepes:

- 4 eggs

- 1 1/2 cups of milk

- 2 cups all-purpose flour

- 6 teaspoons of butter

- 1/4 of a teaspoon of salt

- 1 cup of water

- 2 teaspoons of vanilla extract

For the chocolate mousse:

- 5 ounces of sliced semi-sweet chocolate

- 2 cups melted unsalted butter

- 2 egg yolks

- 1/2 of a cup of sugar

- 2 teaspoons of water

- 2 cups of cold heavy cream

- 1 tablespoon vanilla extract

- Optional: 1 tablespoon coconut rum

For coconut rum cream:

- 1 can Coconut milk

- 3 teaspoons of sugar

- 2 teaspoons of cornstarch

- 2 eggs

- 1/4 teaspoon of salt

- 1 teaspoon of vanilla

- Optional: 2 teaspoons of coconut rum

- 1/2 cup of sweetened shredded coconut

For topping:

- 1 can cold coconut milk.

- 1 tablespoon of powdered sugar

- Toasted coconut for topping

- Toasted coconut rum pecans

Method

1. Place the chocolate in a microwave dish. Microwave at intervals of 1 minute, swirling with each one, until molten and soft. Add the softened butter, and it will thicken. Left to cool aside.

2. Mix the 1 1/2 teaspoons of water, egg yolks, and sugar in a medium saucepan. Place over medium heat on the stove and whisk continuously till the mixture thickens marginally and the edge of a spoon is only brushed around 3-4 minutes. The minute they start curdling and thickening, remember to remove the eggs from the oven. Through the egg mixture, whisk the molten chocolate until fully smooth. Place the cream in the refrigerator as you whisk it. Place the cream in a stand mixer bowl (or use a hand mixer for a large bowl) and whip the cream

until rigid peaks shape. Add (if using) coconut rum and vanilla, and whip when mixed. Be sure that you do not over-beat because the cream can get puffy and butter-like. Now add the cooling chocolate mixture to half the cream. Fold the cream softly into the chocolate till no further stripes are remaining. Add the leftover cream and fold it into the mousse softly. Cover the bowl and put it for 2 hours or overnight in the refrigerator.

3. Mix the cornstarch and coconut milk in a small saucepan. Whisk until you have fully dissolved the cornstarch or no lumps present. Stir in the eggs, butter, salt, and whisk till creamy. Place the pan on the burner and carry it to a boil, continuously stirring. Simmer for about 6 minutes, before the cream thickens and is creamy as pudding. Mix in the coconut rum (if using), vanilla, shredded coconut, and remove from the heat. Place the cream in a bowl, cover it and cool it for 3 hours.

4. In a shallow saucepan, add the butter and heat over low heat. Constantly whisk until brown bits emerge on the rim, around 6-7 minutes, remove from the heat immediately, and set aside. In a blender or food processor, mix the milk, eggs, flour, melted butter, salt, 1 cup of water, and vanilla. For thirty seconds or till just paired, pulse. For about 32 minutes or overnight, place the crepe batter in the fridge. This helps the bubbles die

down, so the crepes would be less prone to break during cooking. The batter will remain for up to 49 hours.

5. Take the batter from the refrigerator and whisk in 1/6 cup of the remaining sugar. Heat a 12-14-inch non-stick skillet over low-medium heat or cast-iron skillet. To coat, sprinkle the cooking spray. In a circular motion, pour 1/6 cup of batter into the skillet. Pick up the skillet quickly using an oven mitt, particularly if a cast iron skillet is used and swirled to distribute uniformly in a circular motion. Cook for 35 seconds and flip. Cook for 15 more seconds, then slice on a work surface. Spread them out flat so that on a sheet of parchment paper, they will cool. Keep working before the batter is out.

6. Place in the freezer the bowl of a stand mixer (or a wide bowl) and the whisk attachment (or beaters).

7. Lay all twenty crepes out on a large clean counter. Remove from the refrigerator the chocolate mousse and the coconut cream and split the mouse and the coconut cream equally between all Twenty crepes (ten with chocolate mousse, ten with coconut cream) and spread in a small, even sheet. Now put one crepe, rotating between both the coconut cream and chocolate mousse. When all the crepes have been used, and the cake is set, please put it in the refrigerator as you whisk the coconut cream.

8. Upside down, turn and free your cold can of coconut milk. About 1/3 cup of coconut water should be on top. Pour it into a jar and reserve it for a different purpose. Scoop the cream out of the coconut and put it in a bowl. Before soft peaks shape, whip the cream. It's not going to be stiff like the usual Beat whipped cream with sugar. Take the cake from the refrigerator and finish with the quantity of coconut whipped cream you want. Return to the refrigerator for 35 minutes or until ready to serve. If needed, when ready to eat, cover the cake with toasted coconut, toasted pecans with rum.

9. Mix two ounces of chocolate and 2 teaspoons of coconut milk in a shallow microwave-proof cup to produce the ganache. Melt the chocolate for 35 seconds in the oven, stirring till the chocolate and coconut milk are smooth. Stir in one tablespoon of vanilla extract or coconut rum.

8. Chocolate Cream Pudding

(Ready in about 30 minutes | serving 6 |Difficulty: Easy)

Per serving: Kcal 282, Fat: 11.8g, Net Carbs: 42.7g, Protein: 4.8g

Ingredients

- 1 cup of white sugar

- 2 teaspoons of cornstarch

- 1/4 teaspoon of salt

- 2 cups of milk

- 2 (1 ounce) chocolate cubes, sliced

- 2 egg yolks

- 2 teaspoons of butter

- 2 teaspoons of vanilla extract

Method

1. Mix the cornstarch, sugar, and salt in a medium saucepan. Stir in the cocoa and milk. Cook, stirring continuously, until the paste thickens and the chocolate melts. Remove from heat and whisk in egg yolks. Return to the heat and simmer for another 3 minutes. Remove from the heat and whisk in the vanilla and butter. Before serving, cool it.

9. Kelly's Butterscotch Pudding

(Ready in about 40 minutes | serving 4 |Difficulty: Easy)

Per serving: Kcal 475, Fat: 18.4g, Net Carbs: 70.4g, Protein: 8.2g

Ingredients

- 1 cup of brown sugar

- 1⁄4 Cup of cornstarch

- 3 Cups of Milk

- 1⁄2 teaspoon of salt

- 3 egg yolks

- 1⁄4 Cup of Butter

- 1 tsp. of vanilla extract

Method

1. Mix the cornstarch, brown sugar, and salt together in a small bowl. Add enough milk to make the paste thick. Bring the milk to a boil in a saucepan over medium heat. Stir in the mixture of brown sugar, put it back to a boil, and simmer for 2 minutes.

2. Place the egg yolks in a shallow saucepan. Temper the yolks in around 1/5 of the heated milk mixture by stirring rapidly. Return the yolk mixture to the hot milk mixture, then return it to the heat. Cook for 2 minutes, stirring constantly; remove from the oven. Stir in the vanilla and butter before the butter is melted. Place them in bowls and let them cool slightly.

10. Fruity Pudding

(Ready in about 25 minutes | serving 7 |Difficulty: Easy)

Per serving: Kcal 207, Fat: 8.2g, Net Carbs: 34.3g, Protein: 0.6g

Ingredients

- 1 (3.5 ounces) instant vanilla pudding mix box

- 1 (8 ounces) frozen whipped topping jar

- 1 (15.25 ounce) can make a cocktail with fruit

Method

1. According to product instructions, cook the pudding; refrigerate until cooled.

2. Fold in the fruit and the whipped topping; cool and eat.

11.   Snow Pudding

(Ready in about 5 minutes | serving 4 |Difficulty: Easy)

Per serving: Kcal 129, Fat: 1.2g, Net Carbs: 27.9g, Protein: 2g

Ingredients

- 6 cups of snow

- 1 cup of milk

- 1⁄2 cup of sugar

- 1⁄2 teaspoon vanilla extract

Method

1. Mix the sugar, milk, and vanilla in a large bowl until well mixed. Stir in the snow cautiously. Freeze and eat directly.

12.   Strawberry Shortcake Ice Pops

(Ready in about 8 hours 10 minutes | serving 8|Difficulty: Easy)

Per serving: Kcal 147, Fat: 4.4g, Net Carbs: 24.2g, Protein: 3g

Ingredients

- 8 vanilla sandwich cookies

- 8 strawberries

- 2 teaspoons White sugar

- 2 teaspoons of water

- 1 (3.4 ounces) box of instant pudding and pie filling cheesecake taste package

- 2 cups of milk

Method

1. Place the cookies in the mixer. Blend on High setting until cookies form fine crumbs, preventing the blender from stirring regularly.

2. Mix the sugar, strawberries, and water in a clean blender. Blend until smooth in a high setting.

3. In a large bowl, mix the pudding mix and the milk. Beat until thick, around 3 minutes, with a blender. Mix in crumbs of cookies.

4. Cover 1/2 full pudding mixture with ice pop molds. Layer to two - thirds complete with strawberry puree; top with remaining pudding mixture evenly. Place molds with sticks, then freeze overnight. If it is challenging to extract pops, run the molds under hot water.

13.   Creamy, Dreamy Vegan Fudge Pops

(Ready in about 3 hours 5 minutes | serving 8|Difficulty: Easy)

Per serving: Kcal 206, Fat: 17.2g, Net Carbs: 15.8g, Protein: 2.7g

Ingredients

- 1 (13.5 ounces) can contain full-fat coconut milk

- 5 teaspoons cocoa powder

- ¼ cup of white sugar

- ¼ cup of new raspberries

- ¼ teaspoon Almond extract

Method

1. In a mixer, whisk together the raspberries, cocoa powder, coconut milk, sugar, and almond extract. Blend on high, around 2 minutes, before the blend is smooth and fluffy like pudding.

2. Using the mixture to fill plastic cups, smoothing over the tips. Insert the sticks into it.

3. Freeze for at least 4 hours until it is firm.

4. Ran warm water over the cups' bottoms before the pops come out quickly.

Chapter 2. New Creations

14.   Peanut Butter Stuffed Chocolate Covered Pretzel Cookies 'n' Cream

(Ready in about 20 minutes| serving 35|Difficulty: Easy)

Per serving: Kcal 30, Fat: 8g, Net Carbs: 12g, Protein: 0g

Ingredients

For Pretzels chocolate covered:

- 40 twists of mini pretzel

- 9 ounces of semi-sweet chocolate or milk chocolate

Peanut butter + cream

- 1/2 cup melted unsalted butter

- 1 2/3 confectioners' sugar

- 1 teaspoon vanilla extract

- 2 teaspoons heavy cream

- Kosher salt

- 3/4 cup of peanut butter

Method

1. Melt the chocolate in the microwave for 35 seconds, swirling until it is soft.

2. You're also required to use a double broiler. Dip each pretzel in chocolate, making it easy to spill off the excess. Put on lined cookie sheets of wax paper and chill until solid, around 15 minutes, in the freezer.

3. Meanwhile, pound the butter in a mixer until smooth and creamy, making the milk filling. Add vanilla and sugar and beat until smooth. Add salt and heavy cream and begin to beat until smooth again.

4. Switch the pretzels over or even cover one pretzel with both the cream filling and one pretzel with the peanut butter to assemble. The pretzels are sandwiched together and set on a baking sheet. They will ooze out, so that's all right. I recommend keeping the pretzels cold so that they do not crack the chocolate. Repeat for the leftover pretzels before you have used both the cookies and fillings. Keep the pretzels in your refrigerator.

15. Hibiscus Cherry and Ginger Beer Ice Cream Floats

(Ready in about 1 hour 15 minutes| serving 4 |Difficulty: Easy)

Per serving: Kcal 165, Fat: 12g, Net Carbs: 27g, Protein: 3g

Ingredients

For hibiscus cherry soda:

- 2 cups of fresh or frozen cherries

- 1/2 cup sugar of coconut or brown sugar

- 1 tsp. Vanilla extract

- 1 cup of water

- 2 teaspoons of dried hibiscus flowers (optional)

- 2 cups of lemon zest

For the floats:

- 2-4 scoops of coconut vanilla bean ice cream or simply vanilla ice cream

- 1/3 cup of hibiscus cherry soda

- 3/4 cup high-quality ginger beer

- 1-2 teaspoons of bourbon or coconut rum (optional)

- Blueberries for serving and cherries

Method

For hibiscus cherry soda:

1. Mix the coconut sugar, cherries, and vanilla beans in a small to medium-sized jar. To mix the cherries up till they are nearly pulp-like, use a muddler or just a fork. Later, you're going to discard them. Place the pot over high heat and add the water. Bring to a boil, sometimes stirring for 6 minutes or so. Remove and add the hibiscus from the heat. Cover for 32 minutes and high. Through a fine mesh strainer, strain the mixture, mix in the lemon juice, and cool until fully cold, around 32 minutes. The syrup should be stored for at least one week in the fridge.

For floats:

1. To each bottle, add a couple of scoops of coconut ice cream. Sprinkle with a few blueberries for some nice color, if needed. Pour the cherry soda over it and cover it with ginger beer. Garnish and enjoy with a raspberry.

16. Firecracker Berry Margarita Floats

(Ready in about 20 minutes| serving 6 |Difficulty: Moderate)

Per serving: Kcal 239, Fat: 17g, Net Carbs: 28g, Protein: 5g

Ingredients

For Margarita (strawberries):

- 1 cup sliced strawberries

- 1/3 cup of honey

- 1 cup of water

- 1/3-1/2 cup of tequila used lemon-lime soda or lime-aid with a non-alcoholic version.

- For a non-alcoholic edition, 2 teaspoons of Cointreau utilizing orange juice

- Just use 1-2 tablespoons of 1/3 cup fresh lime juice if the non-alcoholic option is made.

For Margarita (blueberry):

- 1 cup of blueberries

- 1/3 cup of honey

- 1 cup of water

- 1/3-1/2 cup tequila (lemon-lime soda or a non-alcoholic variant of lime-aid)

- For a non-alcoholic edition, 2 teaspoons of Cointreau utilizing orange juice

- Just use 1-2 tablespoons of 1/3 cup fresh lime juice if the non-alcoholic option is made.

For making the floats:

- Salt

- 3 scoops of vanilla coconut ice cream per person or standard vanilla bean ice cream

For the bean ice cream:

- Lime soda drink

- Fresh strawberries + blueberries

Method

1. In a medium saucepan, mix the sugar, strawberries, and water. Bring to a boil over medium-high heat and cook until the strawberries break down, stirring periodically around 6 minutes.

2. Remove from the heat and beat in a mixer with the mixture. Purée until it's smooth. Alternatively, you should strain the combination using a fine mesh strainer, forcing the juices out of the strawberries. Add the tequila or lemon-lime soda, or orange juice and fresh lime juice, and squeeze the mixture into a small juice jug. Cover until cool or ready to use, then refrigerate.

3. In a medium saucepan, mix the sugar, blueberries, and water. Bring to a boil over medium-high heat and steam until the blueberries soften, stirring periodically around 6 minutes.

4. Remove from the heat and dump in a mixer with the mixture. Purée until it's smooth. Alternatively, you should strain the combination using a fine-mesh strainer, forcing the juices out of the blueberries. Mix the tequila or lemon-lime soda, Cointreau or orange juice, and fresh lime juice and squeeze the mixture into a small juice jug. Cover until cool or ready to use, then refrigerate.

5. Layer two tbsp. Of strawberry margarita with the berries to create the floats, one scoop of ice cream, and 2 tablespoons of blueberry margarita until the glass is almost finished (but leave a little gap top). Pour the water over the surface of the soda until it hits the glass rim.

17.   Five Ingredient Triple-Decker Chocolate Peanut Butter Bars

(Ready in about 45 minutes| serving 16 |Difficulty: Easy)

Per serving: Kcal 353, Fat: 16g, Net Carbs: 26g, Protein: 6g

Ingredients

- 1 stick of salted butter (1/2 cup)

- 1 1/2 cups + 4 smooth peanut butter tsp.

- 2 teaspoons of vanilla extract

- 1-2 cups of sugar confectioners

- 3 cups of chocolate chips semi-sweet or cream

Method

1. Line a circular 8x8 inch pan with parchment paper.

2. Melt 1 1/2 cups of chocolate chips and 2 tsp. of peanut butter in a tiny bowl in the microwave before they are melted. In the prepared pan, pour the chocolate and click against the counter until the chocolate is in an equal layer. Transfer to the refrigerator to schedule for 15 minutes.

3. Meanwhile, pound the vanilla, honey, 1 1/2 cups of creamy peanut butter, and 1 cup of sugar in a large mixing bowl until smooth and creamy. Taste and add more confectioners' sugar of your liking.

4. Over the chocolate plate, spoon the peanut butter mixture into a smooth layer. Transfer to the freezer to schedule for 16 minutes.

5. Melt in the microwave the remaining 1 1/2 cups of chocolate chips and 2 tsp. Of peanut butter before they are melted. Over the peanut butter sheet, pour the sugar, smooth the chocolate out into a smooth layer. Cover and put for one hour or once placed in the fridge. Slice into bars. Hold the bars in the refrigerator for up to one week.

18. No-Bake Triple-Decker Peanut Butter S'mores Bars

(Ready in about 2 hours| serving 16 |Difficulty: Easy)

Per serving: Kcal 348, Fat: 17g, Net Carbs: 28g, Protein: 3g

Ingredients

- 5 entire sheets of graham cracker

- 1 1/2 cups of chocolate semi-sweet chips

- 1 1/2 cups + 2 teaspoons split a smooth peanut butter

- 1/2 cup softened with salted butter, 1 stick

- 2 teaspoons of vanilla extract

- 1 1/4 cups of powdered sugar

- 2-3 bits of split Hershey's Milk Chocolate Bars

- 2 cups of marshmallows

Method

1. Line an 8x8 inch wide parchment paper brownie tray.

2. With graham crackers, line the tray's bottom, cutting the last graham cracker into bits to fit snuggly in the pan.

3. In a small saucepan, add 1 1/2 cups of semi-sweet chocolate chips and 2 tsp. of peanut butter. Heat over low heat, sometimes stirring until smooth and molten. Alternatively, this may be achieved at 35-second intervals in the microwave, swirling for each interval, until melted and smooth. Over the graham cracker layer, pour the chocolate blend and click against the counter until the chocolate is thick and even layer. Cover and put for 35 minutes in the refrigerator to harden.

4. Meanwhile, in a big mixing bowl or bowl of a stand mixer, add a stick of softened butter, vanilla, 1 1/2 cups of smooth peanut butter, and 1 cup of powdered sugar. Beat until creamy and smooth. To your liking, taste, and add more powdered sugar. Spoon the peanut butter mixture into a smooth layer over the chocolate layer. Over the peanut butter sheet, arrange the Hershey's bar bits. Put in the refrigerator for at least 1 hour or 32 minutes in the freezer to firm up.

5. Add the marshmallows to the top of the bars until ready to eat, and toast with a kitchen torch. Alternatively, you can put the marshmallow under the broiler on a parchment-lined baking sheet and toast it for 2-3 minutes. And add them to the top of the bars cautiously. Cut and quickly serve.

19. Grammie's Raspberry Meringue Cookie Bars

(Ready in about 55 minutes| serving 16 |Difficulty: Easy)

Per serving: Kcal 421, Fat: 19.1g, Net Carbs: 59.1g, Protein: 4.7g

Ingredients

- 3 cups All-purpose flour

- 1 1⁄2 cups of softened butter

- 1 1⁄2 cups powdered sugar

- 6 eggs

- 1 1⁄2 cups White sugar

- 2 teaspoons vinegar for rice

- 2 teaspoons cornstarch

- 3⁄4 cup, or to taste, of raspberry

Method

1. Preheat the oven to 175 degrees C.

2. In a large bowl, mix the powdered sugar, flour, butter, and egg yolks. In a 9x13-inch baking sheet, press into the rim.

3. Bake until softly golden in a pre-heated oven, around 14 minutes.

4. Meanwhile, beat the egg whites until foamy with an electric mixer. Add white sugar steadily, proceeding to beat until rigid, shiny peaks develop. Fold the spatula in the cornstarch and rice vinegar.

5. Take the crust out of the oven; coat it with jelly, spoon meringue over the corner. Continue to bake for about 26 minutes until the meringue is nicely browned. Until cutting into bars, leave to cool completely.

20. Chocolate Raspberry Magic Cookie Bars

(Ready in about 1 hour 35 minutes| serving 18 |Difficulty: Easy)

Per serving: Kcal 288, Fat: 17.5g, Net Carbs: 31.4g, Protein: 4.1g

Ingredients

- 1 1⁄2 cups of graham cracker crumbs of chocolate

- 1⁄2 cup of butter, melted

- 1 cup of walnuts sliced

- 3⁄4 cup chocolate black chips

- 3⁄4 cup white chocolate chips

- 1 cup flaked coconut sweetened

- 1 (14 ounces) of condensed milk

- 1⁄3 cup of raspberry preserves without seeds

Method

1. In a small bowl, blend the butter and chocolate graham cracker crumbs. Transfer Onto a 9x13-inch baking tray. Sprinkle generously with the walnuts on top. Cover it with dark chocolate chips, almonds, and white chocolate chips.

2. Drizzle uniformly sweetened condensed milk over a sheet of coconut. Place tablespoons of raspberry preserve on top, so until baked and sliced, there will be some on each bar.

3. Bake in the preheated oven for 28-30 minutes until softly golden. Let it cool for around one hour before finishing. To render 18 bars, split them into 6 columns and 3 rows.

21. Spring Sugar Cookie Bars

(Ready in about 39 minutes| serving 16 |Difficulty: Easy)

Per serving: Kcal 195, Fat: 11.2g, Net Carbs: 23g, Protein: 2.2g

Ingredients

- Cooking spray

- 1 (16.5 ounces) refrigerated sugar cookie dough box

- ½ cup of almonds

- 2 ½ teaspoons of apricot preserves

- 2 ½ teaspoons of peach preserves

- 2 teaspoons of dried strawberry

- ½ tsp. Honey

- ½ cup of chocolate semisweet chips

Method

1. Preheat the oven to 175 degrees C. With cooking oil, gently spray a 9x13-inch baking sheet.

2. Press on the lined baking sheet with the cookie dough.

3. Bake in the preheated oven for 9 to 10 minutes until golden brown. Remove the crust and leave it to cool for 6 minutes or so.

4. On a baking sheet, spread the almonds.

5. In the preheated oven, toast for 12-15 minutes before the almonds begin to turn golden brown and become fragrant. Let it cool momentarily and chop into the size you like.

6. In a bowl, mix the strawberry preserves, apricot preserves, peach preserves, and honey. Spread in the skillet over the cookie dough. Lightly scatter the almonds over the preserves.

7. In a microwave-safe cup, melt chocolate chips at 16-second intervals, stirring 1 to 2 minutes after melting. Drizzle the almonds with melted chocolate. Keep the chocolate on for another 6 minutes. It's sliced into bars.

22. White Chocolate and Candied Fruit Magic Cookie Bars

(Ready in about 40 minutes| serving 12 |Difficulty: Easy)

Per serving: Kcal 463, Fat: 26.5g, Net Carbs: 52.3g, Protein: 6.2g

Ingredients

- Cooking spray

- 1 1⁄2 cups of vanilla wafer crumbs

- 1⁄2 cup of butter, melted

- 1 (14 ounces) condensed milk may be sweetened (such as Eagle Brand ®)

- 1 cup (such as Ghirardelli ®) white chocolate chips

- 1 cup of Candied Red and Green Cherries

- 1 cup of walnuts sliced

Method

1. Preheat the oven to 175 degrees C. Using cooking spray to coat a 9x13-inch baking sheet.

2. In a cup, combine the vanilla wafer crumbs and the melted butter. Within the prepared baking tray, press the crumb mixture onto the bottom. Pour the condensed sweetened milk generously over the crust. Layer uniformly on top of candied cherries, chocolate chips, and walnuts. For a fork, push down hard.

3. Bake in the preheated oven for 28-30 minutes until finely browned. Loosen when wet, from the sides of the plate. In the bowl, let it cool; cut into squares.

23. My Five Candy Bar Cookies

(Ready in about 1 hour 50 minutes| serving 36 |Difficulty: Easy)

Per serving: Kcal 314, Fat: 16.8g, Net Carbs: 37.8g, Protein: 6.8g

Ingredients

- Cooking spray

- 2 (16.5 ounces) rolls of refrigerated cookie dough with peanut butter

- 1 cup of peanut butter

- 1 cup Crushed pretzels

- 1 cup of salted peanuts sliced

- 1 (14 ounces) of condensed milk

- 1 (14 ounces) box of caramels

- 1 package of chocolate chips (12 ounces)

Method

1. Preheat the oven to 175 degrees C. With cooking spray, oil a 9x13-inch baking dish.

2. In a dish, mix 1/3 cup peanut butter, 1 tube of cookie dough, and pretzels. In the prepared baking dish, push onto an even plate.

3. Bake until only golden in the preheated oven and placed 13- 14 minutes. Enable slightly to cool.

4. In a dish, mix the remaining tube of cookie dough, the remaining peanut butter, and 1/3 cup of peanuts. Press the scale of the baking dish in an even layer onto a sheet of parchment paper. For around 30 minutes, refrigerate until solid.

5. Preheat the oven to 175 degrees C. In a saucepan, mix the condensed milk and caramel over medium heat. Cook for about 6 minutes, constantly stirring, until smooth. In the baking dish, spill over the cookie dough crust and scatter in an even layer. Cover with the combination of refrigerated cookie dough, then peel the parchment paper off.

6. Bake in the preheated oven, 26 to 28 minutes, until golden brown. Enable slightly to cool.

7. Pour the chocolate chips into an oven tray; heat until smooth, around 2 minutes in the microwave. Stir in 2/3 cup of peanuts left and scatter over cookie bars.

24. To-Die-For Brownie Chocolate Chip Cookie Bars

(Ready in about 1 hour 9 minutes| serving 20 |Difficulty: Easy)

Per serving: Kcal 336, Fat: 17.4g, Net Carbs: 39.7g, Protein: 5.2g

Ingredients

For brownies:

- 2⁄3 cup of flour all-purpose

- 3⁄4 cup cocoa powder unsweetened

- 1⁄4 teaspoon of salt

- 1⁄4 teaspoon baking powder

- 3⁄4 cup of white sugar

- 4 coffee-flavored liqueur fluid ounces (Optional)

- 2 eggs

- 1 teaspoon of vanilla extract

- 1⁄2 cup of butter

For peanut butter cookies:

- 1 1⁄3 cups of flour

- 3⁄4 teaspoon of baking soda

- 1⁄2 teaspoon baking powder

- 1⁄4 teaspoon of salt

- 1⁄2 cup of crunchy peanut butter

- 1⁄2 cup unsalted, softened butter

- 1⁄2 cup of brown sugar

- 1⁄2 cup White sugar

- 1 egg

- 1 teaspoon of vanilla extract

- 2 (4 ounces) bags of white chocolate, cut into bits or to taste, such as Baker's®

Method

1. Preheat the oven to 175 degrees C.

2. In a large bowl, mix 1/4 teaspoon salt, 2/3 cups of flour, cocoa powder, and 1/4 teaspoon baking powder.

3. In a large bowl, stir together 2 eggs,3/4 cup sugar, coffee liqueur, and 1 teaspoon vanilla extract. Add the melted butter and flour mixture; add the batter to an ungreased 9x13-inch baking pan; stir and scatter.

4. In a large bowl, sift together 1/2 teaspoon baking powder, 1 1/3 cups of flour, baking soda, and 1/4 teaspoon salt.

5. Using an electric mixer to mix brown sugar, peanut butter, unsalted butter, and 1/2 cup of white sugar in another dish. Beat in the vanilla extract with 1 egg and 1 teaspoon. Stir in a blend of flour. Place the peanut butter cookie dough in the baking pan on top of the brownie mixture.

6. Bake in the preheated oven for 16-18 minutes until the cookie coating is golden brown. Leave for 16 minutes to cool. Split into squares and leave to cool entirely in the pan for around 22 more minutes.

7. Put the white chocolate in a microwave-proof bowl. Heat in the microwave for about 32 seconds before it is molten. Put the molten chocolate in a plastic sandwich bag and cut a very tiny hole in a section. Drizzle over the cooling cookie brownies with white chocolate.

25. Fudge Jumbles (Chocolate Cookie Bars)

(Ready in about 50 minutes| serving 24 |Difficulty: Easy)

Per serving: Kcal 322, Fat: 14.1g, Net Carbs: 44.5g, Protein: 4.8g

Ingredients

- 2 1⁄2 cups of flour

- 2 cups brown sugar

- 1 cup of margarine

- 2 eggs

- 2 teaspoons vanilla extract

- 1 teaspoon of baking soda

- 3 cups of oats

- 3⁄4 cup chips of butterscotch

- 3⁄4 of a cup of chocolate chips

- 2 teaspoons Margarine

- 1 (14 ounces) of condensed milk

- 2 teaspoons vanilla extract

Method

1. Preheat the oven to 175 degrees C. Grease a 9x13-inch tray for cookies.

2. In a dish, add the 2 teaspoons of vanilla extract, flour, brown sugar, 1 cup of margarine, eggs, and 1 teaspoon of baking soda once blended. Stir the oats in. 2/3 of the mixture is pushed onto the bottom of the prepared plate.

3. In a saucepan over medium heat, melt the chocolate chips, butterscotch, and 2 teaspoons of margarine. Stir in the vanilla extract with condensed milk and 2 teaspoons until creamy. Load the remaining oat mixture into the baking pan, crumble on top.

4. Bake in the preheated oven for around 20 minutes until set. Cool for 12 minutes at the very least. Sliced into squares.

26. Almost-Candy Easy Bar Cookies

(Ready in about 30 minutes| serving 24 |Difficulty: Easy)

Per serving: Kcal 284, Fat: 14.7g, Net Carbs: 34.9g, Protein: 3.8g

Ingredients

- 1 (18.25 ounce) Devil's food cake mix

- 1/2 cup of softened margarine

- 1 (14 ounces) condensed milk

- 1 cup of butterscotch chips

- 1 cup of chocolate chips

- 1 of a cup of coconut

- 1/2 cup of sliced walnuts to taste

Method

1. Preheat the oven to 175 degrees C.

2. In a bowl, blend the margarine and devil's food cake mix and until crumbly. Press the mixture gently into a 9x13-inch baking tray. Pour the condensed, sweetened milk over the crust. Sprinkle with chips of butterscotch, chocolate chips, walnuts, and coconut.

3. Bake for 22-25 minutes in a pre-heated oven until the coconut has browned. Let it cool down and slice into squares.

27.   Hershey's Chocolate Candy Bar Cookies

(Ready in about 35 minutes| serving 24 |Difficulty: Easy)

Per serving: Kcal 242, Fat: 12.6g, Net Carbs: 30.9g, Protein: 2.5g

Ingredients

- 2 ¼ cups of flour

- 1 teaspoon salt

- 1 teaspoon of baking soda

- 1 cup of butter

- ¾ cup of packaged brown sugar

- ¾ cup of white sugar

- 1 teaspoon of vanilla extract

- 2 eggs

- 8 (1.5 ounces) bars (such as Hershey's®) milk chocolate candy bars

Method

1. Preheat the oven to 190 degrees C. Prepare a 9x13-inch baking tray with butter.

2. In a dish, mix the salt, flour, and baking soda.

3. In a separate bowl, mix the white sugar, butter, brown sugar, and vanilla extract. Whisk in one egg at a time. Slowly blend the sugar mixture into the flour mixture. Spread 1/2 of the dough uniformly into the packed pan.

4. Bake until partly firm, around 12 minutes, in the preheated oven.

5. Using chocolate bars to cover the partly baked dough, breaking up if needed to match. Slide the remaining dough as equally as possible over the chocolate. Bake in a hot oven till golden brown, for an extra 10-12 minutes.

Chapter 3. Classic Biscuits

28. Ginger Biscuits

(Ready in about 30 minutes | serving 20 |Difficulty: Easy)

Per serving: Kcal 117, Fat: 5g, Net Carbs: 17g, Protein: 1g

Ingredients

- 100g salted butter

- 75g Light brown sugar

- 1 tbsp. of grated ginger

- 100g of gold syrup

- 250g Flour

- 1 1/2 tbsp. of ground ginger

- 1 tsp. bicarbonate soda

- 1 tiny yolk of an egg

Method

1. Heat the oven to 190C/170C. Line two large baking pans with parchment for baking. Melt the golden syrup, sugar, butter, and fresh ginger in a saucepan over medium heat and allow to cool.

2. In a cup with a wooden spoon, combine the flour, ground ginger, and baking soda. Stir the egg yolk and cooled sugar mixture in steadily and knead lightly to create a dough.

3. Roll into balls of 20 g and place 3 cm between each on the baking trays to allow for spreading. Bake until golden brown for 8-10 mins. Leave to cool for a minute on the trays, then move to a wire rack to cool completely.

29. Vegan Shortbread

(Ready in about 40 minutes | serving 14 |Difficulty: Easy)

Per serving: Kcal 176, Fat: 9g, Net Carbs: 21g, Protein: 2g

Ingredients

- 250g flour

- Caster sugar 75g

- ½ tbsp. cornflour

- 1 tsp vanilla extract

- olive oil 160ml

Method

1. In a food processor, whizz the starch, sugar, a pinch of salt, and the cornflour to sieve and blend briefly, then add the vanilla and drizzle in the olive oil, pulsating the blades of the food processor until you get a smooth, golden dough. Cover and relax for 30 mins.

2. Preheat oven to 180C/160C, and put parchment paper on a baking tray. Roll the dough out to a thickness of 5 mm on a thinly floured work surface and use a circular or fluted cutter, around 6 cm in diameter, to cut out circles of shortbread. Switch to the baking sheet using a thin sharp knife. It can be frozen on the baking tray and, when firm, moved to a box. It would last up to three months.

3. Sprinkle 1 tbsp. Of sugar over the biscuits and bake until golden brown for 15-20 mins. Leave to cool to firm up on the tray for a couple of minutes, then move to a cooling rack to cool completely.

30. Gingerbread Cookies

(Ready in about 32 minutes | serving 20 |Difficulty: Moderate)

Per serving: Kcal 135, Fat: 5g, Net Carbs: 20g, Protein: 1g

Ingredients

- 120g unsalted butter

- 1 1⁄2 tbsp Black treacle

- 170g Brown sugar

- 1⁄2 tsp. sea salt

- 1 egg

- 200g Flour

- 1⁄4 tsp soda bicarbonate

- 1⁄4 tsp. of ground cloves

- 1 1⁄2 tsp ginger

- 1⁄2 tsp cinnamon

- 60g Golden caster sugar

Method

1. In a big mixing cup, beat the brown sugar, honey, treacle, and salt together. Add the egg and beat in all the other dry ingredients, except the caster sugar. In the freezer, cool the mixture for 1 hr.

2. Preheat the oven to 200C/180C. Line 2 baking sheets with parchment for baking. Roll the mixture (weighing for consistency, if you like) into twenty even-sized balls. On a small pan, tip the caster sugar, add balls, and roll around just to coat. On the baking sheets, spread each ball out. Bake until golden brown for 9-10 mins. On a wire shelf, allow cooling completely.

31.   Anzac Biscuits

(Ready in about 35 minutes | serving 20 |Difficulty: Easy)

Per serving: Kcal 118, Fat: 7g, Net Carbs: 13g, Protein: 1g

Ingredients

- 85g of oat porridge

- 85g desiccated coconut

- 100g Flour

- 100g Caster sugar

- 100g butter

- 1 tbsp. of gold syrup

- 1 tsp. soda bicarbonate

Method

1. Preheat the oven at 170C in a cup, placed the almond, oats, flour, and sugar. In a shallow pan, warm the butter and mix in the syrup. Add 2 tbsp. Of boiling water to the soda bicarbonate, then whisk in the syrup and butter.

2. Create a well and dump the golden syrup and butter mixture into the center of the remaining ingredients. To mix the dry ingredients, gently stir.

3. To make space for spreading, put a dessertspoonful of the mixture on greased baking sheets, around 2.7cm/1in apart. Bake for 8-12 mins in batches until brown. Move to cool to a wire shelf.

32. Simple Jammy Biscuits

(Ready in about 22 minutes | serving 12 |Difficulty: Easy)

Per serving: Kcal 170, Fat: 8g, Net Carbs: 25g, Protein: 2g

Ingredients

- 200g Self-rising flour

- 100g Caster sugar

- 100g of butter

- 1 egg

- 4 tbsp. of strawberry jelly

Method

1. Preheat the oven to 200C. Mix the sugar, flour, and butter, so the mixture looks like breadcrumbs. You may, instead, do this in the mixing blender. To shape a stiff dough, add enough eggs to stick the mixture together.

2. Flour your hand and form the dough, around 5 cm in diameter, into a tube. Cut into slices of 3cm thickness and put on a broad baking sheet. Space them out, as when baking, the mixture can spread.

3. Create a slight indentation with the end of a spoon in each piece's center and drop a teaspoon of jam in the middle. Bake until slightly elevated and just golden, for 10-12 mins.

33. Basic Biscuit Dough

(Ready in about 20 minutes | serving 30 |Difficulty: Easy)

Per serving: Kcal 118, Fat: 7g, Net Carbs: 13g, Protein: 1g

Ingredients

- 250g of butter

- 140g Caster sugar

- 1 egg yolk

- 2 tsp vanilla extract

- 300g flour

Method

1. In a large bowl, mix the sugar and butter with a wooden spoon, add the vanilla extract and egg yolk, and stir briefly.

2. Add the flour and swirl until the paste is well mixed. To make it a very nice mix and push the dough together, you might need to bring your hands in at the top.

34. Pistachio and Cranberry Cookies

(Ready in about 30 minutes | serving 2 |Difficulty: Easy)

Per serving: Kcal 140, Fat: 9g, Net Carbs: 15g, Protein: 2g

Ingredients

- 175g of sugar

- 85g Golden caster sugar

- 1⁄2 tsp vanilla extract

- 225g Flour

- 75g Pistachios

- 75g cranberries

Method

1. Use the wooden spoon to mix the sugar, butter, and vanilla extract. You would need to get your hands in at this point to put the mix together as a dough, mix in the flour, then dip in the pistachios and cranberries. Halve the dough and form it into a log about 6cm from each part. Cover in cling film and freeze for up to 4 months or chill for 1 hour.

2. Preheat the oven to 190C. Cut the logs into circles 2 cm wide, put them on a cookie pan lined with baking parchment, and bake for 15 minutes.

35. Custard and White Chocolate Biscuits

(Ready in about 30 minutes | serving 25 |Difficulty: Easy)

Per serving: Kcal 132, Fat: 6g, Net Carbs: 18g, Protein: 1g

Ingredients

- 140g of butter

- 175g Caster sugar

- 1 egg

- 1/2 tsp vanilla extract

- 225g of self-rising flour

- 85g Custard powder

- 85g White chocolate

Method

1. Preheat the oven to 190C. Line 4 baking sheets with parchment for baking. In a food processor, bring the butter and sugar in and whizz till light and fluffy. Add the vanilla and egg, and blend properly. Sift the flour and custard powder together, then dump into the mixer and

blend it into a dough with a pulse. Scrape out the stick blender and work side by side with the chocolate.

2. A little bigger than a walnut, roll the dough into balls, then put on the baking trays, a tiny bit apart to allow for spread. In your hands, push each biscuit down lightly.

3. Bake until softly golden, for 15 mins.

36. Freezer Biscuits

(Ready in about 30 minutes | serving 30 |Difficulty: Easy)

Per serving: Kcal 138, Fat: 8g, Net Carbs: 16g, Protein: 2g

Ingredients

- 200g butter

- 200g light brown sugar

- 2 eggs

- 1 tsp vanilla extract

- 200g Self-rising flour

- 140g oats

- Your choice of flavors

- 50g of sliced nuts including pecans, hazelnuts, or almonds

- 50g desiccated coconut

- 50g raisin or blended berries

Method

1. Mix the sugar in butter when it is soft. Beat together before the sugar is blended in, utilizing an electronic hand whisk or working some arm muscle. Beat the eggs one at a time, accompanied by the vanilla extract and a touch of salt if you prefer. Stir in the oats and flour. At this point, the mixture will be very rigid. Now consider what else you would like to incorporate and stir with some or more of the flavors.

2. Tear off a greaseproof layer of the sheet. In the middle of the board, pile up half the mixture and then use a spoon to scatter the mixture thickly down the center of the page. Pull one edge of the sheet over it and roll it up until the cylinder is secure. If you have difficulty making it smooth, then move it around a kitchen surface like a rolling pin. To be about the width of a cup, you'll need it. Twist-up the ends until it is securely packed and then put it in the freezer. It can be frozen for 3 months.

3. Preheat the oven to 180C for cooking and unpack the frozen biscuit mixture. Break off a disc around ¼cm in length with a sharp knife. Dip the blade into a cup of hot water if you have trouble slicing through it. Cut as many biscuits off as you need, so for another day, pop the blend back into the fridge. Put on a baking sheet, spreading them wide as the mixture expands while baking, then cook till the tops are golden brown for 15 minutes. Leave to cool before eating for at least 5 mins.

37. Double Chocolate Shortbreads

(Ready in about 32 minutes | serving 10 |Difficulty: Easy)

Per serving: Kcal 290, Fat: 18g, Net Carbs: 31g, Protein: 3g

Ingredients

- 175g of sugar

- 85g Golden caster sugar

- 200g Flour

- 2 tbsp. powder of cocoa

- 100g Chocolate chips

Method

1. Using a spoon, blend the sugar and butter. Mix in the flour and cocoa, followed by the chocolate chips. At this point, you will need to mix it with your hands. Halve the crust and roll each slice about 6cm thick into a log. Cover for sixty minutes or many days in cling film and cool. It can be frozen for 1 month.

2. Preheat the oven at 190C, switch to a cookie sheet lined with parchment paper, and bake for 12 mins. Slice logs into 2cm-thick circles.

38. Unicorn Biscuits

(Ready in about 35 minutes | serving 20 |Difficulty: Easy)

Per serving: Kcal 136, Fat: 7g, Net Carbs: 17g, Protein: 2g

Ingredients

- 250g Flour

- 150g of butter

- 100g Caster sugar

- 1 egg

- ½ tsp vanilla extract

- Pink food color

- 50g sugar icing

- 1 lemon juice

Method

1. Using your hands, rub the flour and butter together until it looks like breadcrumbs, then add a sprinkle of salt. Mix the egg, sugar, and vanilla extract in another dish, and spill it over the butter and flour mixture. Knead it

together carefully, then split the dough into 2 equal pieces. In one of them, knead some pink food coloring and leave the other white. In sheets of cling film, cover all forms of dough and chill in the fridge for 25 mins.

2. On a gently floured surface, roll the simple dough out until it is around 26cm long by 21cm thick. For the pink dough, do the same and lay one on top of the other. Move gently with your rolling pin across the surface once or twice enough to press close. Trim all the edges off so that they are smooth, then roll them up carefully from one of the short edges to create a strong spiral. Cover securely and cool for 1hr or overnight in cling film.

3. Heat oven to 182C/162C fan/gas 4 with baking parchment and line 3 trays. Unwrap the dough, cut the end, cut the rest into 22 slices, and place it on your prepared baking tray with the cut side down. Bake at the very edges for 20 mins or until ever so slightly golden. Before moving them to a wire shelf, let them cool on the tray.

4. To build the consistency of smooth peanut butter, blend the icing sugar with sufficiently lemon juice and dump the sprinkles into a small bowl. Dip the biscuits' outside sides into the icing (or use the back of a teaspoon to

scatter it over the edges) and then into the sprinkles, turning to cover.

39. Angry Biscuits

(Ready in about 30 minutes | serving 40 |Difficulty: Easy)

Per serving: Kcal 110, Fat: 6g, Net Carbs: 13g, Protein: 1g

Ingredients

- 200g Unsalted butter

- 350g flour

- 50g of cocoa powder

- 200g Golden caster sugar

- 1 egg

- ½ tsp vanilla extract

- 100g dark chocolate chips

For decorating:

- 50g of dark chocolate

- 50g of white chocolate

- 1-2 stem ginger pieces

- Chili pinch flakes

- Pinch flakes of sea salt

Method

1. Mix the butter and flour in a large bowl together until small breadcrumbs are visible in the mixture, then whisk in the cocoa powder. Beat the egg, sugar, and vanilla together in another bowl until creamy, then add in the flour and butter. To form a reasonably soft pastry, knead it together with your hands and then knead it into the chocolate chips. For 35 minutes, cover in cling film and cool in the fridge.

2. Heat oven to 130C/120C fan/gas 3 with baking parchment and line 2 baking sheets. On a lightly floured board, put the resting dough and roll it out to around the thickness of a £1 coin. Slice into shards with a knife or cut into bits. So equally bake the biscuits, aim to make sure they're around the same size; ours were between 7-8cm long and 4cm tall. Feel free to re-roll as soon as you like the dough so that you can use it all up.

3. Place the biscuit pieces on your prepared trays and bake for 15-17 mins in the oven; you will need to do this in 2

lots. Remove from oven and leave to cool until the parchment is cut until decorating, cause it to cool fully on a wire rack.

4. Place the chocolate in different microwaveable bowls to decorate and heat each one in thirty-sec microwave bursts until melted, alternatively placed the bowls over barely simmering water pans until the chocolate is fully melted. Spread out all the baked biscuits on the parchment paper sitting close together and scatter the molten chocolate across the surface using a teaspoon, spill, drizzle, or break.

Chapter 4. No Quite Cookies

40. Chocolate Dipped Viennese Whirls

(Ready in about 1 hour | serving 25 |Difficulty: Easy)

Per serving: Kcal 204, Fat: 13g, Net Carbs: 19g, Protein: 2g

Ingredients

- 250g unsalted butter

- 75g icing sugar

- 250g Flour

- 50g cornflour

- 60g hazelnuts

- 1 tsp vanilla extract

- 300g dark chocolate

Method

1. Preheat the oven to 195°C/fan 175°C/gas 5. Line 2 large baking sheets with paper for baking. In a food processor, mix all the ingredients except for the chocolate until creamy.

2. Spoon the mixture into a piping bag equipped with a wide-open star nozzle, then pipe on the prepared baking

sheets with swirls and 'S' shapes. Bake until pale golden, for 13-14 minutes. Cool for 6 minutes on the sheets, then gently placed to cool on a wire rack.

3. Into the molten chocolate, dip half per biscuit, then leave on baking paper to harden.

41. Amish Sugar Cookies

(Ready in about 25 minutes | serving 72 |Difficulty: Easy)

Per serving: Kcal 85, Fat: 4.8g, Net Carbs: 9.7g, Protein: 1g

Ingredients

- 1 1/2 cups of vegetable oil

- 1 1/2 cups white sugar

- 2 eggs

- 4 cups All-purpose flour

- 1 teaspoon of baking soda

- 1 teaspoon Baking powder

- 1 cup of buttermilk

- 3/4 teaspoon of salt

- 3⁄4 teaspoon vanilla extract

Method

1. Preheat the oven to 170 degrees C.

2. Mix the vegetable oil, the sugar, and the eggs. Mix the baking powder, baking soda, flour, buttermilk, salt, and vanilla with the mixture.

3. On baking sheets, pour teaspoon-sized volumes of batter, allowing plenty of space between each one. These cookies are going to puff up and get tall.

4. For 10 minutes, bake them.

42. Grandma Tibbitts Sugar Cookies

(Ready in about 30 minutes | serving 24 |Difficulty: Easy)

Per serving: Kcal 228, Fat: 9.3g, Net Carbs: 33g, Protein: 3g

Ingredients

- 1 cup of lard

- 2 cups white sugar

- 2 eggs

- 1 cup of buttermilk

- 4 cups All-purpose flour

- 1 teaspoon of baking soda

- 1 teaspoon nutmeg

- 1 salt teaspoon

Method

1. Preheat the oven to 200 degrees C (400 degrees F). Cookie sheets of grease.

2. Mix the lard and sugar together in a bowl. One at a time beat the eggs, then whisk in the buttermilk. At this point,

the mixture will be very runny. Mix the baking soda, starch, nutmeg, and salt; use a wooden spoon to whisk into the buttermilk mixture by hand. Try not to over-mix the dough because it would be dense with the cookies. Place a spoonful on the cookie sheets that have been packed. The dough can be kept in the fridge for a couple of hours for cut-out cookies. Roll the cookie-cutter between each cut to a thickness of 1/4 inch and flour.

3. Bake in the preheated oven for between 10-12 minutes. Enable cookies to chill for 6 minutes on a baking sheet before shifting to a cooling rack completely.

43. Buttermilk Cookies

(Ready in about 26 minutes | serving 36 |Difficulty: Easy)

Per serving: Kcal 157, Fat: 6.4g, Net Carbs: 22.3g, Protein: 2.4g

Ingredients

- 1 Cup shortening

- 2 cups white sugar

- 4 eggs

- 4 cups All-purpose flour

- 4 tablespoons of baking powder

- 2 tablespoons of baking soda

- 1 salt teaspoon

- 1 cup of buttermilk

- 4 teaspoons of vanilla extract

Method

1. Preheat the oven to 220 degrees C (425 degrees F). Cookie sheets of grease.

2. Mix the shortening and the sugar in a bowl. Beat the eggs, then whisk in the vanilla, one at a time. Mix the starch, baking soda, baking powder, and salt and whisk variously with the buttermilk into the creamed mixture. Place a rounded spoonful on the cookie sheets that have been prepared.

3. Bake in the preheated oven for 8-10 minutes. Enable cookies to chill for 5 minutes on a baking sheet before transferring to a wire rack to cool fully.

44. Brown Sugar Drops

(Ready in about 1 hour 30 minutes | serving 72 | Difficulty: Easy)

Per serving: Kcal 73, Fat: 3.1g, Net Carbs: 10.7g, Protein: 0.9g

Ingredients

- 1 cup shortening

- 2 cups of brown sugar prepared

- 2 eggs

- 1/2 cup of buttermilk

- 3 1/2 cups of all-purpose flour

- 1 teaspoon of baking soda

- 1 teaspoon of salt

Method

1. Mix the brown sugar and shortening together in a big bowl until creamy. Beat the eggs one at a time, then add the buttermilk. Mix the baking soda, starch, and salt; whisk until well mixed in the buttermilk mixture. For at least one hour, cover the dough and chill.

2. Preheat the baking oven to 205 degrees C. Prepare Cookie sheets with Oil. Drop the dough on the ready cookie sheets with a rounded teaspoonful two inches apart.

3. Bake in a pre-heated oven for 10-12 minutes, until almost no impression is left when touched by your finger. Remove directly from the cookie sheets to cool on wire racks.

45. Sugar Cookie Cutouts

(Ready in about 1 hour 40 minutes | serving 36 |Difficulty: Easy)

Per serving: Kcal 135, Fat: 6.1g, Net Carbs: 18.4g, Protein: 1.8g

Ingredients

- 1 cup of butter

- 1 cup of white sugar

- 2 eggs

- 1 teaspoon vanilla extract

- 3 ¾ cups all-purpose flour

- 2 tablespoons of baking powder

- ¼ cup of whipped cream

- ½ cup colored sugar for decoration

Method

1. Add the butter and the sugar together in a medium dish. Stir in the vanilla and shells. Sift the flour and baking powder together and blend alternately with the heavy cream into the creamed mixture. Cover the dough and chill until firm for 3-4 hours.

2. Preheat the oven to 170 degrees C. Prepare cookie sheets of grease.

3. Roll out the dough to a thickness of 1/2 inch on a well-floured board. Using cookie cutters, carve into ideal forms. Put cookies on the prepared cookie sheets 2 inches apart. If needed, sprinkle with colored sugar.

4. Bake for 13-15 minutes in the preheated oven until the cookies' edges are light brown. Remove from the baking sheet and cool on the racks with wire. Store in an airtight jar.

46. Thick Cut-Outs

(Ready in about 1 hour 23 minutes | serving 75 | Difficulty: Easy)

Per serving: Kcal 148, Fat: 6.4g, Net Carbs: 21.1g, Protein: 1.8g

Ingredients

- 2 1/8 cups White sugar

- 2 cups butter

- 4 eggs

- 6 egg yolks

- 1 1/2 teaspoons Vanilla extract

- 7 cups All-purpose flour

- 1 tablespoon baking powder

- ½ teaspoon of salt

- 4 Cups of Confectioners' Sugar

- ¼ cup of vegetable oil

- 1 tablespoon of hot water

Method

1. Mix the sugar and butter in a big bowl until creamy. Beat in the eggs and egg yolks, mixing well after each one at a time, in a vanilla extract mix. Stir in the sugar mixture, then mix the baking powder, flour, and salt. Cover and cool the dough for at least 2 hours.

2. Preheat the furnace to 190 degrees C (375 degrees F). Cookie sheets of grease. Roll the dough out to 1/2-inch-thick on a floured surface, then use cookie cutters to cut into ideal shapes. On the lined baking sheets, placed 2 inches apart.

3. Bake in the preheated oven for between 9-10 minutes. Enable the cookies to cool for 6 minutes on the baking sheet before shifting them to a wire rack.

4. Mix the oil, confectioners' sugar, and 2 teaspoons of vanilla until smooth to produce frosting. Add sufficiently hot water progressively to obtain a spreadable strength. Spread over warm cookies.

47. Soft Gingerbread Cookies

(Ready in about 3 hours 45 minutes | serving 36 |Difficulty: Easy)

Per serving: Kcal 75, Fat: 0.8g, Net Carbs: 15.8g, Protein: 1.2g

Ingredients

- ¾ cup of molasses

- ⅓ cup of packaged brown sugar

- ⅓ Cup of Water

- ⅛ cup of butter

- 3 ¼ cups of flour all-purpose

- 1 teaspoon of baking soda

- ½ teaspoon allspice field

- 1 teaspoon ginger

- ½ teaspoon of cloves field

- ½ teaspoon cinnamon

Method

1. Mix the brown sugar, molasses, water, and butter in a medium bowl until smooth. Mix the baking soda starch, allspice, ginger, cloves, and cinnamon, whisk them into the wet ingredients until all of the dry is absorbed. Cover and cool the dough for 2 hours.

2. Preheat the oven to 170 degrees C. Roll the dough out to a thickness of 1/2 inch on a well-floured board. In the desired shapes, take off. Put cookies on ungreased baking sheets 2 inches apart.

3. Bake in the preheated oven for between 10-12 minutes. Remove to cool on wire racks from the cookie sheets.

48. Coconut Icebox Cookies

(Ready in about 2 hours 30 minutes | serving 24 |Difficulty: Easy)

Per serving: Kcal 118, Fat: 1.3g, Net Carbs: 17g, Protein: 5g

Ingredients

- 1⁄2 cup of butter

- 1 cup of white sugar

- 1 egg

- 2 teaspoons vanilla extract

- 1⁄2 teaspoon extract of coconut

- 1 3⁄4 cups of all-purpose sifted flour

- 3⁄4 teaspoon of salt

- 1⁄2 teaspoon of baking soda

- 1 cup coconut

Method

1. Add the butter until smooth; add the sugar and continue to cream until fluffy and light. Stir in the flavoring of the vanilla, egg, and coconut.

2. Mix the flour with the baking soda and salt. The flour mix and the shredded coconut are alternately applied to the creamed mixture. Shape the dough into logs with a diameter of around 3 inches. Cover the dough firmly and cool for 2 hours or overnight.

3. Preheat the oven to 195 degrees C. Take the dough out of the fridge and cut it into 1/6-inch slices. Bake on an ungreased baking sheet for around 12 minutes, until the edges are golden on a wire rack, cool.

49. Christmas Cookies I

(Ready in about 35 minutes | serving 144|Difficulty: Easy)

Per serving: Kcal 177, Fat: 4.8g, Net Carbs: 32.2g, Protein: 2.4g

Ingredients

- 4 cups molasses

- 2 cups of butter

- 1 teaspoon salt

- 2 teaspoons of ground cloves

- 2 teaspoons of allspice

- 2 teaspoons of anise oil

- 3 cups dry currants

- 2 cups Sour milk

- 6 cups White sugar

- 4 eggs

- 2 teaspoons Cinnamon

- 4 cups of walnut halves

- 2 teaspoons of nutmeg

- 3 Cups of Raisins

- Package of 1 (8 ounces) candied citron peel

- 1 tablespoon baking soda

- 16 cups All-purpose flour

Method

1. Cook the molasses and sugar till the sugar dissolves. Let syrup cool in a bowl.

2. Crush the raisins, currants, almonds, and citron and combine in a large bowl with the butter. Add the cooled sugar to it.

3. Blend the spices, salt, anise, eggs, and sour milk.

4. Mix the soda and flour. Place the dough in the fridge for some days.

5. The dough may well be rolled out and trimmed or molded and sliced into rolls. Place them on greased sheets of cookies.

6. Bake for 15 to 20 minutes at 175 degrees C. On wire racks, cool it.

50. Chewy White Chocolate Chip Gingerbread Cookies

(Ready in about 1 hour 30 minutes | serving 24 |Difficulty: Easy)

Per serving: Kcal 231, Fat: 11.1g, Net Carbs: 31.2g, Protein: 2.4g

Ingredients

- 3/4 cup of butter

- 1 cup of white sugar

- 1 egg

- ¼ cup of molasses

- 2 cups All-purpose flour

- 2 teaspoons of baking soda

- 1 teaspoon ginger

- 1 teaspoon cinnamon

- ½ teaspoon of cloves

- ½ of a teaspoon of nutmeg

- ½ teaspoon of salt

- 1 (12 ounces) white chocolate chip box

Method

1. In a mixing bowl, whisk together the butter and one cup of sugar till the mixture is smooth, and stir in the beaten egg and molasses. Whisk together the baking soda, flour, ginger, cinnamon, garlic, nutmeg, and salt in another bowl; whisk the flour mixture into half a cupful of the molasses mixture. Stir in the chips with the white chocolate. Refrigerate dough for at least one hour.

2. Preheat the oven to 170 degrees C.

3. Scoop up a generous dough spoonful and roll it up into a ball. Roll the ball of sugar, put it on an ungreased baking sheet, and gently flatten it. If needed, sprinkle a little sugar on the cookie. For the remainder of the sweets, repeat.

4. In the preheated oven, bake the cookies until well browned, for 10 minutes. Allow for around 2 minutes to cool on the baking sheet before moving to cool on the racks.

Conclusion

The different recipes for cookies, cakes, pies, brownies, fudges, ice pops, biscuits, and others that we present in this cookbook were designed to make your celebrations, holidays, birthdays, or any other special occasion, a memorable moment with your loved ones, offering them the opportunity to enjoy delicious sweets that will delight even the most varied tastes. You will be able to create recipes based on chocolate, coffee, peanut butter, nuts, raisins, oatmeal, honey, and many other ingredients that will allow you to become an expert in baking cookies and their varieties.

The variety of cookies that exist is due to the difference between them, in which the ingredients differ as well as the way of preparation and baking method, which gives a differentiation of the cookies in terms of consistency, shape, flavor, texture. Achieving different types of cookies is the hobby of many bakers, who seek to create unique cookies in their style.

CPSIA information can be obtained
at www.ICGtesting.com
Printed in the USA
BVHW051351270421
605941BV00002B/179